SKILLFU

MW01123700

An Interactive Guide To Raising Great Kids

Lyn Vinnick Kaller

Maria LaPadula Perez

University Press of America,® Inc.
Lanham · New York · Oxford

Copyright © 2002 by
University Press of America,® Inc.
4720 Boston Way
Lanham, Maryland 20706
UPA Acquisitions Department (301) 459-3366

12 Hid's Copse Rd.
Cumnor Hill, Oxford OX2 9JJ

ISBN 0-7618-2334-4 (paperback : alk. ppr.)

Table of Contents

Acknowledgments

The authors wish to acknowledge the contributions of several skillful parents whose sharing of real-life experiences we greatly appreciated: Debby and Peter Tesler; Sarah and Andy Chamlin; Tory Dietel-Hopps and Jonathon Hopps; Sarah and Richard Watkins; Karyn and Barry Kurland; Kim and Mark Cheiken; Kathie and David Mandel; and our parents, Helene and Leonard Vinnick; Irene Bongiorno and Jack LaPadula. Their honesty and candid opinions on parenting helped bring this guidebook to life.

We warmly thank our husbands, Seth Kaller and Edward Perez, whose constant support and guidance encouraged us to complete this book. We lovingly acknowledge our daughters, Jordana Marelle Kaller and Lauren Nicole Perez, who have challenged us to enhance our own parenting skills.

Chapter 1

Introduction

As a parent, you are probably "good" at all kinds of things, especially blaming yourself when your child misbehaves, feeling guilty about punishing negative behavior, and getting frustrated and stuck. As clinical psychologists who have had the opportunity to work with many different children and families, we hear one thing over and over again: "I can't seem to stop the battles with my child! I've tried everything and so far nothing has worked—I'm at the end of my rope! I just don't know what else to do!" Sound familiar?

One of the most important jobs in our society is raising the next generation well. One parent said to us recently, "The hardest thing about parenting is hoping I'm parenting my children in a way that helps them develop a strong sense of self...to lead happy adult lives. A difficult part of parenting is not being sure that I'm always doing the right thing." There are all kinds of manuals out there for all kinds of situations—manuals for learning to drive a car; computer training manuals; manuals to teach us to play a musical instrument. There are graduate schools that teach law, medicine, and other specialties. *But when is the last time you saw a manual or degree in "parenting?"* There is no formal training for parenting. Just because you have a piano doesn't mean you know how to play the piano; likewise, having a baby doesn't mean you automatically know how to parent effectively. Don't feel guilty if you aren't a parenting expert—how would you be? We wrote this book to give parents, primary caregivers, teachers, and other professionals who work with children an interactive guide to more effective parenting.

Parents use many methods to get their children to behave: rewarding them, spending special time together, using "time-out," taking things away, and ignoring. *But when is the last time you truly felt what it is like to be successful and empowered?*

Often, parents get stuck—what they are trying doesn't work as well as it could. Many parents today feel powerless, a process that usually begins early on and manifests itself as ineffective discipline or lack of supervision.

Some of the signs that you are "stuck":

- You're yelling or getting frustrated more than usual for you.

- Your child continues to misbehave even after you've tried some technique to make things better.

- There's a change in your child's school performance.

- There's a change in your child's social behavior, like withdrawing from friends or social activities.

Several years ago, we facilitated a landmark research program aimed at decreasing behavior problems in children by working with the child, family, and parents. We became interested in sharing the parent training component of the program when we recognized that parents could absolutely affect the way the children were behaving, and in such positive ways! Research suggests that one of the key ingredients to changing children's behavior problems quickly is to change what parents are doing. You, as a parent, may have little or nothing to do with why your child is having problems or how the problems got started. But by focusing on structure, better communication, and effective problem-solving, you can help get yourself and your child back on track and help to increase your child's healthy emotional development.

This book covers *seven basic parenting skills:*

- Keeping Yourself Calm and in Control (chapter 2)

- Co-Parenting and Parenting Support (chapter 3)

- Choosing Your Battles (chapter 4)

- Keeping Your Child Calm and in Control (chapter 5)

- Communicating Effectively (chapter 6)

- Problem-Solving Effectively (chapter 7)

- Enhancing Positive Behavior (chapter 8)

These interactive parenting skills build on each other; they are like laying the foundation for a new home before you build the walls or the roof. For example, before you learn to keep a child calm, you must first be able to remain calm and in control yourself. Likewise, a prerequisite to solving problems effectively is for everyone to be calm, and to communicate respectfully. So don't skip ahead here. It is important to tackle one skill at a time, and in this particular order.

When you finish reading this book you should:

1. Be able to deal more effectively with problems a child presents.

2. Be aware of skills you could learn and further develop.

3. Know when it's time to seek professional help.

Parenting Pretest

Below is a parenting quiz to give you a sense of your skills. You should answer these questions before you read any further. Please be honest with yourself. When you finish the quiz, add up your score using the Scoring Key.

Never	Rarely	Sometimes	Frequently	Always
0	1	2	3	4

How often do you feel frustrated when you
discipline your child?   _____

How often do you want more time just for yourself?   _____

How often do you say things to your child
that you later regret?   _____

How often do you and your spouse/partner disagree
about how to raise the children?   _____

How often do you feel undermined by another adult
when you discipline your child?   _____

How often do you wish you had more time with your
spouse/partner to talk about parenting issues?   _____

How often do you have more than three parenting
dilemmas at the same time about your child?   _____

How often do you wish you could deal with parenting
dilemmas more effectively?   _____

How often do you give advice to your child without
being asked for it?   _____

How often do you "lecture" to your child—that is, talk
for at least one minute without stopping?   _____

How often do you say you're going to punish your
child and then give in?   _____

How often does your child lose his/her temper or
become easily frustrated while you are trying to
discipline him/her?   _____

How often do you get into power struggles with
your children?   _____

How often do you spend less than one hour a day in
conversation with your child?   _____

How often does your child interrupt you and not give
you a chance to explain yourself?   _____

How often do you consider parent-child communication
to be important in your family?   _____

How often do you speak with your child when he/she is
not quite calm enough to listen to you?   _____

How often do you fail to effectively and completely
solve problems with your child?   _____

How often do you come up with only one or two
solutions to a problem? _____

How often do you forget to focus on your child's strengths? _____

How often is it difficult to spend special quality time
with your child for 15 minutes a day? _____

Scoring Key:
0 – 30
You are a parenting expert. You may find some other helpful hints in this book, and ways to practice and continue what you are already doing well. Congratulations!

31 – 50
Though you know a great deal about interactive parenting, there are some areas where you could improve your skills.

51 – 70
You may find that you are getting stuck fairly often in your parenting. This book will help you get back on track quickly and effectively.

71 – 84
HELP! Parenting is a challenge for you right now, but it doesn't have to always be that way. This book should help you feel better about yourself and your relationship with your child, and give you some tips to improve your parenting skills. Don't give up!

Understanding Behavior Problems in a New Way

Before we talk about specific parenting skills, it's important to understand what "behavior problems" are—how they come about, what initiates and maintains children's behavior problems, and what kinds of things protect children from developing problems.

Think about your own family. *Why is it that your children are so different from each other?* Please take a moment to write down three characteristics about each of your children—for example, having an easy temperament, being friendly or gregarious, or having low tolerance for frustration.

Child's Name: _____

Three characteristics that describe my child are:

_____

_____

_____

Child's Name: _____

(if you have a second child)

Three characteristics that describe my child are:

_____

_____

_____

Child's Name: _____
(if you have a third child)
Three characteristics that describe my child are:

_____

_____

_____

As we mentioned, children are different for different reasons. *But why does one child have problems, while another does not?* First, it is difficult, if not impossible, to talk about what "makes" a child have problems or what "causes" them—because we can't do experiments on our children. But what we do know is that behavior problems come about for a variety of reasons and in a multitude of ways.

Usually, behavior problems develop along a continuum. Your child may start out being a relatively "easy" baby, then have some *mild temper tantrums.* Over time these outbursts can become more unmanageable. As the child gets older, tantrums turn into *defiance* and even *aggression* sometimes. Left untreated, behavior problems can lead to more chronic problems such as substance abuse, poor school performance, ongoing rejection by peers, and difficulty with a job in adulthood. That is why it is so important to catch problems early on and to do something about them.

Children may develop behavior problems as a result of many behavioral, psychological, or social factors. The list below can help you evaluate how these factors relate to your child. This is not a comprehensive list, nor is it meant as a checklist, but it will give you some things to consider when you are trying to understand your child even better than you already do.

We are born with certain *biological factors*—such as having a difficult infant temperament, a learning disability, or a physical health problem—that can exacerbate a behavior problem.

Which biological factors might contribute to your child's behavior problems?

_____

_____

There are also *psychological factors* that children are exposed to in their early years that are associated with more behavior problems. These factors might include experiencing a stressful life event such as the parents' divorce; having parents who are not supervising or monitoring regularly or who are emotionally rejecting, inconsistent, negative, or uninvolved; or living in a large-sized family.

Which of these psychological factors might contribute to your child's behavior problems?

_____

_____

Finally, there are *community or social factors* that might contribute to the development or maintenance of a child's problems—for example, having limited family communication, having two parents who work outside the home, having only a few extracurricular activities with peers, having chaotic family schedules, or lacking social support from adults.

Which of these social factors might contribute to your child's behavior problems?

_____

_____

Now that you are more aware of things that can make problems *worse*, we want you to concentrate on making the problems *better*. There are a host of things that protect children from ever developing a behavior problem or that can make a problem improve quickly.

Below are some biological, psychological, and social factors that help children develop in a healthy way. Again, this is not meant as a comprehensive checklist but rather as a list of things you might consider when you are trying to understand your child even better than you already do.

We are born with certain *biological factors* that protect us. These would include having a happy infant temperament, being physically healthy, and having no learning problems.

Which of these biological factors might have protected your child from having more serious behavior problems?

_____

_____

There are also *psychological factors* that children are exposed to in their early years that are associated with helping them develop emotionally in a healthy way. These include having good self-esteem, coping well with stress, having parents who communicate realistic appreciation and encouragement, having parents who are involved and supervising well, and being able to express feelings easily.

Which of these psychological factors might contribute to protecting your child from behavior problems?

_____

_____

Finally, there are *community or social factors* that contribute to the development or maintenance of health in children—for example, having two or more hobbies, having several extracurricular activities, having positive peer and family relationships, and having a caring adult involved in the child's life.

Which of these social factors might help to protect your child from developing behavior problems?

_____

_____

Keep these protective factors in mind. You may want to refer to them as you read through other chapters of this book. It is important to *consider your child's strengths* as you try to decrease any problems you're having.

Let's summarize:

1. Behavior problems in children can range from mild to severe and can come about for a variety of reasons.

2. If what you're doing isn't working, it's time to practice some skills in this book.

3. Focus on your child's strengths—they protect children from developing more severe behavior problems.

4. You have the ability to change your child's behavior—even though what you have done in the past may not have "caused" the problems to develop in the first place.

Chapter 2

Keeping Yourself Calm and in Control

You will notice that, in general, intense feelings can escalate and aggravate a situation. We are all human, and when we experience any type of strong or intense feeling, it will influence our behavior. Parents are people, too. When you have intense feelings, it gets in the way of your being able to think clearly and act rationally. Many types of situations can create strong emotions and frustrations. For example, as a parent, you want to implant values in your children that they will carry into adulthood. Some parents are afraid that if they don't do this now, their child will never become the wonderful human being they have spent so much time raising and nurturing. Also, as your children get older they may start to test and reject some of your values, and they may be trying to find out things on their own, which can be very frustrating. Because there are so many situations that cause parents to feel frustrated, it is extremely important for parents to learn to calm down before they put their skillful parenting into practice. Keeping yourself calm is the first skill this book discusses, because it is the foundation for the other skills. Parents have to learn how to keep themselves calm before they can go on to master the other skills in this book.

Step 1. Catch yourself getting angry and calm down.

The first step is to catch yourself getting angry **RIGHT AWAY** and to calm down **RIGHT AWAY**. That means that you should not let your anger escalate to the point that you are beyond calming down and thinking clearly. *If you are already angry, you waited too long.* This sounds like a simple statement, but it is extremely difficult for parents to catch their anger soon enough. Usually, you feel that anger just happens and you don't even see it coming. This may be true, but it is very important to pay more attention to how you get angry and to try to control it so that you can deal with your children in a calm manner. As parents, we don't want to discipline our children when we are too angry, because our strong feelings can cause us to do things we will later regret. For example, when parents become exasperated, they resort to saying things like, "What's happened to you? You used to be such a sweet child."

Step 2. Connect your thoughts with your feelings.

Okay, so at this point most parents can see that the first step is understanding that they should stay calm when dealing with their children. But you are probably asking yourself **"HOW?"** Well, there are several ways you can calm yourself down. One way is to CONNECT YOUR THOUGHTS WITH YOUR FEELINGS. How we think about a situation influences our feelings and mood. Self-control comes about when you realize that thoughts and feelings are connected. For example, if you **THINK** your child is mean and selfish, you'll **FEEL** disappointed and angry that you have a child like that. On the other hand, if you **THINK** that your child has some problems that you can tackle together, you'll **FEEL** calm and helpful. We cannot emphasize enough that to deal effectively with your child you must first observe yourself. This means being aware of your moods and how they affect your child's behavior, because your child reacts to your behavior and mood all the time. It is very important for parents to practice this skill. First we will give you some examples of how this works, and then we want you to try it on your own.

Parent's Thought About Child's Behavior	**Parent's Feeling About Child's Behavior**
1. He's mean and selfish and always has to have his own way.	1. Anger, hurt, depression
2. She's just a spoiled brat!	2. Disappointed that she's my child
3. He's not able to do the things he wants and so he acts out; I'll need to help him in this situation.	3. Calm and helpful

Now you try it. Think about some situations that have occurred recently with your child. Write down the first thoughts that come to your mind about your child's behavior in the space provided below. Then write down how you feel about this behavior. Practice this a few times, and you will see how your thoughts and feelings are connected.

Thoughts About Your Child's Behavior

1. _____

2. _____

3. _____

Feelings About Your Child's Behavior

1. _____

2. _____

3. _____

Step 3. Use self-talk to establish self-control.

Another way parents can keep themselves calm is to USE SELF-TALK. Self-control comes about when you recognize that the things you say to yourself (self-talk) are connected to how you feel and behave. It will make a big difference in your mood if you can say calming things to yourself. The reason is that WHAT WE SAY, HOW WE FEEL, AND HOW WE BEHAVE ARE ALL CONNECTED. Here are some examples of a parent's upsetting self-talk and then some examples of what a parent's calming self-talk could be. After you have read these examples, it will be your turn.

Parent's Upsetting Self-Talk	**Parent's Calming Self-Talk**
1. I'm so angry I could scream!	1. Be consistent. It will get better.
2. This is too much work. I can't handle this.	2. Take one day at a time. It will get easier.
3. This child will NEVER get better.	3. My child did not develop these problems all at once, and he/she won't get better all at once. Be patient.

Now you take some time to practice this skill. First write down some examples of **upsetting** self-talk that you sometimes use. Then, write down some examples of **calming** self-talk that you could use in the future.

Upsetting Self-Talk

1. _____

2. _____

3. _____

Calming Self-Talk

1. _____

2. _____

3. _____

Step 4. Reframe or use humorous exaggerations.

Reframing and using humorous exaggerations are two other ways that parents can help themselves remain calm. These are two effective, non-hurtful ways for you to express anger and frustration. You can either focus on the good things about a situation so that it is not so disturbing to you ("reframe") or you can use humorous exaggeration of your feelings. By using these techniques you are not saying that your child's behavior is okay; you are getting your own emotions under control and providing a non-hurtful response.

Let's try **reframing** first: When you ask your child about his day, he yells, "It's not your business and leave me alone." Using reframing, you could tell him, "I can see that you are trying to assert your independence." You see, you got your emotions under control, you focused on the positive aspect of the situation, and you can still impose a consequence for his rude tone of voice if you wish to.

Now let's try **humorous exaggeration.** When using this technique you are using humor to make light of the situation. Remember, you can use this technique as long as you are not dealing with a very serious problem. For example, your daughter arrives home half an hour past her curfew. Tell her jokingly and with a smile: "The next time you come in after curfew, I'll ground you so long you'll think you're Rip Van Winkle by the time you see daylight again."

Now you try it. Use the space provided below to describe a situation, and then give an example of a reframe or a humorous exaggeration.

Child's Behavior

_____

Reframe

_____

Humorous Exaggeration

_____

Child's Behavior

_____

Reframe

_____

Humorous Exaggeration

_____

Child's Behavior

_____

Reframe

_____

Humorous Exaggeration

_____

Step 5. Learn to relax.

Another way you might try to stay calm is to practice getting better at relaxing. You might use some of the relaxation methods described below if you want to really work at staying calm.

First, you can use the Muscle Relaxation Technique. The important elements are learning to put tension and then relaxation into the muscle groups throughout your body. You should practice this technique twice a day. You need to follow this procedure deliberately, meaning that you do it on purpose and with some degree of pacing and control. Rushing through this procedure will only defeat its effectiveness.

Here's how to practice the Muscle Relaxation Technique:

- Sit in a straight-backed chair, erect, feet flat on the floor, with hands loosely in the lap. Or you may choose to relax while lying on your back.

- Be sure to choose a place where you can remain quiet and undisturbed for about 15 minutes.

- Next, you have to learn how to tense your muscles. You must hold each set of muscles tense for several seconds and take note of what it feels like to be tense. Then you must relax each set of muscles so that you know what a true state of relaxation feels like.

- At the end of all these exercises, conjure up a vision of total body relaxation.

Tense, then relax the following muscle groups: forehead, eyes, nose, lips, jaw, neck/shoulders, right fist/arm, left fist/arm, right foot/leg, left foot/leg, buttocks, stomach.

TENSE AND RELAX EACH BODY PART. THEN REPEAT THE WHOLE SEQUENCE. THEN JUST SIT IN A RELAXED POSITION FOR FIVE MINUTES.

If this procedure just is not for you, don't despair. There are a lot of other ways you can relax. For some people, deep breathing is very relaxing—or walking, listening to music, exercising, or taking warm baths. It does not matter which technique you use as long as you are able to relax. What is important is that, when you feel yourself getting really upset, you try to create enough distance to calm down and then, in a less emotional way, address your child's unacceptable behavior. **Remember to keep a cool head.** Try some ways that you think will help you to feel relaxed and write down your evaluation of each one (was it successful?).

Relaxation Method:

1. _____

2. _____

3. _____

Evaluation of Relaxation Method:
(Not Helpful; Somewhat Helpful; Very Helpful)

1. _____

2. _____

3. _____

We realize that all of this sounds much easier than it actually is. But many of the parents we have worked with over the years have said that once they learned how to keep themselves calm, they were much better able to deal with their children. It will get easier with time and practice. Being able to handle intense and strong feelings differently will benefit you in many ways. It will help you get your emotions under control, think more clearly, and tolerate frustration better. In addition, it will help you to model calm behavior for your child. We know that children learn a great deal by observing and watching others, especially their parents. If you can model calm behavior for your children, they learn that when they get frustrated and angry they should stay calm, instead of learning that when people get frustrated and angry they should yell, scream, or hit.

Before you go on to the next chapter, take some time to practice this new skill of keeping calm. Practice one attitude change (your thoughts or self-talk) and one behavior change (reframing, humor, or relaxation exercise) when in a conflict situation, before you read the next chapter.

As you start to practice this skill, you may have difficulty and start to doubt yourself as a parent, doubt your abilities to make changes, and feel overwhelmed and stuck. Remember that you will not learn these skills overnight. It will take some time. Just reading this book is a step in the right direction. You will start by making small changes, and keep in mind that as you make these small changes you are heading in the right direction and you will see bigger changes along the way. Also, as you go on to learn other skills, you can always go back to a chapter to review a skill or spend extra time on a particular skill. Be patient, and remember that change is possible as long as you are making an effort.

CHAPTER 3

Co-Parenting and Parenting Support

By now we hope you have practiced the various ways of calming yourself down when you get angry and frustrated. Now we want to discuss another important part of skillful parenting called **co-parenting**. In order to parent your child effectively, you will need to be able to work together with your spouse/partner and learn how to negotiate. Also, parents need to be able to seek support from their spouse/partner and not undermine each other's efforts. Parenting should be seen as a team effort.

We are not saying that you have to agree with your spouse/partner about every aspect of parenting. In fact, many parents will disagree about parenting strategies. It is all right to each have a specific way of parenting your child, as long as you can negotiate the differences. So if you and your spouse/partner disagree on some aspect of parenting, it is crucial that you discuss it and negotiate your differences. It is important that parents work together and present a united front to the children. Respecting each other's ideas will facilitate better parenting. On the other hand, not agreeing and not discussing your parenting differences can create conflict in your relationship. If you stop for a moment to think about it, there are probably times that you and your spouse/partner have worked together to discipline your child versus when you've felt undermined by the other parent. Was it easier to deal with the situation when you worked together? Did you get a better result when you worked as a team? Take a moment to think about a baseball team that has co-coaches. The players need to know what to do while they play the game. If the coaches don't work together, communicate, and negotiate, the players will not be able to play to the best of their abilities. Think of parenting as being similar to the ways coaches have to work together for the good of the team.

Now take some time at home to discuss the following issues. First of all, each parent should describe what he/she needs and/or wants from the spouse/partner while co-parenting. For example, one parent may want the spouse/partner to stop giving her disapproving gestures while she is disciplining the children. Another parent may want his spouse/partner to be next to him while he is disciplining the children but not to say anything. Once the parents have had a chance to talk about what they want from each other, they should discuss how often this behavior actually occurs. If the answer is "not often enough," it is time to spend more energy on co-parenting.

It is also extremely important for parents to discuss their philosophy on raising and disciplining children. It would be best if people discussed this before they actually became parents, but that does not always happen. Don't despair. It is never too late for parents to start discussing these issues. Parents can start by discussing these topics: Do you agree on how to reinforce your children's positive behavior and how to punish negative behaviors? Do you believe in nonviolent means of discipline? What are your ideas on sharing parenting and household responsibilities? These are just examples of the issues that are important for parents to discuss at home. You will probably have no difficulty adding to our list.

Take a few moments to list some of the issues that you and your spouse/partner feel are important to discuss further at home:

1. _____

2. _____

3. _____

Up to this point we have been talking about parents working together. Sometimes there is only one parent who is responsible for raising and disciplining the children. For *single parents* it is very important to learn how to *seek another adult's support and guidance.* Don't think you have to do it all alone. You should take some time to think about who is capable of helping you co-parent and decide whom you would want to co-parent with. For example, some single parents co-parent with someone they are dating, a friend, or a relative. Once single parents find someone they can talk to about parenting issues, they feel much more relaxed and better able to cope with some of the stresses of parenting alone.

It is also important for all parents to take care of themselves individually and as a couple so that they are able to be better parents. Parents sometimes have to be helped to identify other sources of life satisfaction besides parenting. This will help them gain more energy to manage their children, and it will help them feel better about their lives. The following are some suggestions:

- Spend time away from children, doing adult activities such as hobbies, community activities, or quality time with a spouse/partner.

- Spend time alone to relax, unwind, and take a break (read, take a bath, exercise, listen to music).

Can you think of three satisfying activities for yourself?

1. _____

2. _____

3. _____

It is important for parents to remember that life is like a pizza. There is a slice for your duties as a parent, a slice for your children, a slice for your job, and a slice for you as an adult. It is this last slice that so many parents forget about. But how can you be a skillful and effective parent without first being a happy, content, and satisfied adult?

Chapter 4

Choosing Your Battles

On to the third parenting skill. It is imperative that you know how to "choose your battles" with your child. This means that you have to set priorities and focus on which of your child's behaviors are really important, dangerous, and in need of attention and which ones you can let go of for now. This is what choosing your battles is all about. Setting priorities will free up your energy to focus on other important issues.

Sometimes children themselves can teach us what to discipline and what to laugh about, what is a priority and what is not. For example, a three-year old girl was hopping in a little swimming pool her parents set up, and then rolling in the dirt. She was covered with rocks, sand, and dirt from head to toe. Her mother asked what she was doing, and the child said, "Mom, don't you know? This is what kids do!"

Other times it is less clear how we should proceed. The mother of a five-year-old boy described this problem: Her son broke one of her favorite candy dishes while he was playing ball in the house, and the housekeeper saw him do it. Her son threw away the pieces and told no one. When confronted, he said his cousin did it. It took a day and a half before he finally told the truth. *As a parent, would you deal with the ball-throwing problem first, or the lying problem first?* Here's where choosing your battles comes into play.

Choosing battles can be challenging. You're probably asking yourself: "Okay, but how do I set priorities?" Parents should decide ahead of time what to discipline in terms of a child's disruptive behaviors and what to leave alone. We will discuss some guidelines for you.

First, answer this question:

If you had five wishes, which five problems would you solve?

1. _____

2. _____

3. _____

4. _____

5. _____

So now you have five problems listed. Not all of these problems can be solved at one time. Let's go through the following steps to put your five problems in priority order.

Which of these problems is the most dangerous?
If your children are exhibiting dangerous behaviors—that is, behavior that could physically harm themselves or someone else—it is crucial that these behaviors be at the top of your list. If your child is exhibiting any dangerous behaviors, please list them here.

1. _____

2. _____

If you are dealing with a *dangerous* problem, your priorities are set! You must address dangerous problems first. Go ahead and read the next chapter. If you *don't* have a dangerous child on your hands at this time, continue reading this chapter.

Which of the problems on your list are most disruptive to family life?
Go back to your original list. The next important factor in setting priorities is to think about which behaviors are most disruptive to family life. Many parents prefer to focus on problems that are disruptive to the day-to-day functioning of their family, especially when a problem is affect-

ing other family members. Which of the five problems listed above disrupt family life the most?

1. _____

2. _____

3. _____

Which behaviors can you as a parent actually control?

It is sometimes difficult for parents to accept that they cannot control all of their children's behaviors. For example, you can tell your child, *"No playing Game-Boy at home while you're doing homework."* But if your child is at a friend's home to study for a test, there is no way that you can control Game-Boy playing.

Of the three disruptive problems you just listed, which two do you feel you can control?

1. _____

2. _____

Which behaviors can you monitor and measure?

When you are setting priorities, we want you to be sure that the behavior in question is something you can see and keep track of. For example, if the behavior is something you can monitor, you would be able to tell friends about it and they would have no trouble picturing this problem in their minds. Think about how often the problem occurs, under what circumstances, and when the problem does not occur.

For example, saying that your child is rude is *not* a problem you can monitor or measure, because it is too vague. Being rude could mean that the child talks back, looks away when spoken to, or uses inappropriate language. It is very important to be specific about the problem you are describing.

Of the two behaviors that you can control, which one could you easily monitor and measure?

1. _____

This is the problem you would put at the top of your list of priorities to solve with your child.

Once this problem is solved, you can go back and solve the second most important problem. Remember, keep on focusing on your child's strengths while you set priorities for problem areas.

If you are still having trouble:

If setting priorities is still difficult for you, you are not alone! Something that helps parents put problems in priority order is to break them down into tiny parts. Problems don't go from A to B in a linear way; they happen in a cyclical way. We want you to try to think of problems in terms of what happens *minute to minute,* each separate interaction, so that the problem is not so overwhelming.

Take a look at the "Cycle of Relationships" on the next page. Problems become more manageable once they're broken down into parts.

Cycle of Relationships

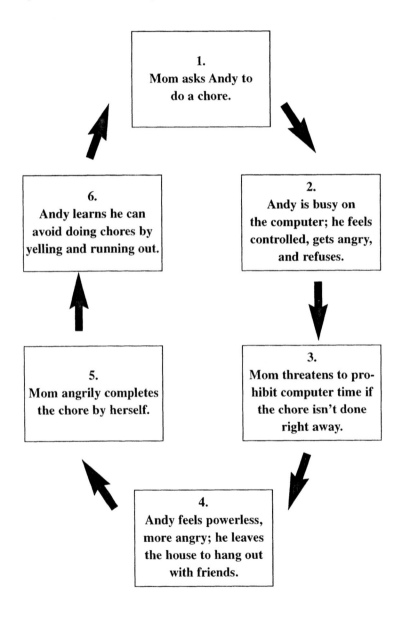

Here, everyone in the family plays a part in the problem, and we could intervene or make changes in more than one place. For example, maybe next time Mom won't ask Andy to do the chore right away, but she will ask him to do it sometime in the next few hours. Or, if Andy knew how to handle his feelings of frustration better, maybe he would talk about chore responsibilities with his mother. We don't know what role Andy's father plays in this because he was not mentioned.

Here is a blank "Cycle of Relationships" for you to complete. Practice breaking down a problem that you have with your child.

Cycle of Relationships Exercise

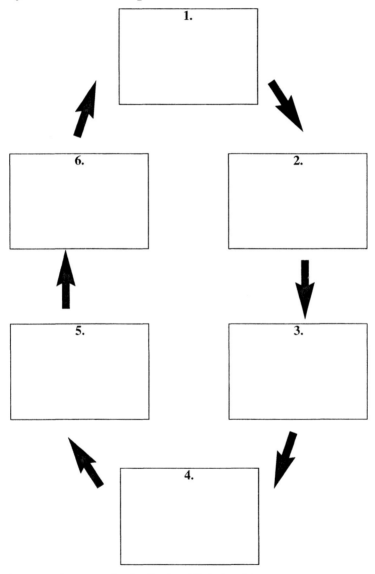

Once you have practiced a Cycle of Relationships, you can go on to a Choose Your Battles exercise.

Choose Your Battles Exercise

Read each of the following situations carefully. If you are doing this with your spouse/partner, you should each *independently* put the problems in order, from the most important problem to the least important problem. Then discuss whether you agreed or disagreed on which problems were important, and discuss the pros and cons of each parent's decision.

Rank Order

_____You walk into your 12-year-old child's room and find a pack of cigarettes under the dresser.

_____The principal calls from school to tell you that your 10-year-old child started yet another fight in school today.

_____You've been negotiating a curfew and your 14-year-old has consistently returned home 20 to 30 minutes later than the hour you both agreed on.

_____Whenever you have company over to the house, your 13-year-old becomes more oppositional and talks back rudely to you in front of the company.

_____You can never seem to get anything done in the evening because your 17-year-old is always yelling and fighting with his/her younger siblings in the living room and you feel you have to go in and break up the fights.

Now that you know how to break a problem down into parts, you can decide what part is most problematic for you and your family, and tackle *that* part. At the very least, you should be able to pick your top three problems.

By this time, most parents have begun to view problems at home from a broader perspective. In addition, they understand the roles they play in ongoing cycles of difficulty and conflict with their children. Therefore, parents may begin to doubt themselves and their abilities to make changes, and they may feel incompetent. Also by now, parents feel that they are putting in a lot of time in trying to solve problems, and they may feel angry about this. It is important to remember that change is possible if parents work hard; that even though they may not have created the problem, they can resolve it. *Keep up the good effort!*

Chapter 5

Keeping Your Child Calm and in Control

Now that you have read about, and practiced, staying calm, handling your own strong feelings, co-parenting, and choosing your battles, you are ready for the next step. You can now be a model, a teacher, to help your child calm down and to *break the cycle of hostility* in your family. In general, strong feelings like anger, frustration, or sadness get in the way of our children being able to think clearly and behave appropriately. No, it is not your fault that your child is having a fit. But as a parent you can possibly (never definitely) intervene in such a way that your child will calm down and feel better.

In this chapter you will learn to enhance a child's ways of dealing with strong feelings. But first, let's review what makes your children explode and whether you really can intervene to make the situation better. Think about situations that bring on very intense emotions for children. This may include times when the child is in a power struggle with someone, arguing with a sister or brother, losing a turn in a game, being asked to obey a rule, or getting a bad grade on a test.

What are three situations that generally lead to a very strong reaction (usually anger or frustration) in your child?

1. _____

2. _____

3. _____

Now that you have identified these "trigger" situations, keep them in mind. *Remember, the first step to changing anything is to be aware of it.*

Here we will review four basic strategies to help your child calm down.

Step 1. Listen.

How many times today did you listen to your child, without interrupting, offering advice, or lecturing? Often, simply *listening* can help children calm down. This is the first and easiest strategy. Listening doesn't mean you believe or agree with your child. Instead, it means you are interested and being supportive. Children begin to control their anger better when they feel that adults listen to them.

If you listen, and your child is telling you something bad, you can still set a consequence later on. The most important thing is to be sure you let your child know, by listening, that you are empathic to his/her position.

In today's busy and complex world, it is very important to make sure you set aside time to talk. That does not mean you have to hold a formal meeting. Sometimes the best discussions take place while you are driving the car or making dinner. Children will talk if they know you are going to listen to them. If your children know you are listening, they are more likely to trust you enough to talk about everything in their life. Because some children find it difficult to talk to their parents about important issues that really matter, parents have to pay special attention to what their children may be trying to say. It helps to pay particular attention to emotions—not just to the emotion itself, but also to its intensity. In addition, remember that children like being asked their opinions. So a good way to get your child talking is to ask his/her opinion. Also, don't forget to give your child a chance to explain himself/herself. Even if you think you know what children are going to say, let them explain themselves anyway.

Let's practice. Here are some examples and a chance for you to try listening even better.

Child's Disruptive Behavior
After she has been rejected for a potential summer job, your daughter comes home and knocks over a pile of books on the table.

Parent Listens and Responds
"It's hard to be rejected. Let's talk about it in the den. I'm sorry it didn't work out this time." (Then set a limit on knocking over the books by asking her to clean the whole den.)

Your son comes home from school with a cut on his chin, clearly having been in a fight after school.

"Must have been a rough day. I'm here if you want to talk about it. I'm concerned about your chin." (Then follow up with the school about it.)

NOW YOU TRY IT:

My Child's Disruptive Behavior

1. _____
2. _____

How I Listened and Responded

1. _____
2. _____

Step 2. Set a positive tone.

Remember the "Cycle of Relationships" that you completed in chapter 4? The way you respond to your child affects the way he/she responds to you. It's like a cycle that you set up. As a parent, you set the tone of the situation by what you say and do. Your child's emotions and behavior will reflect yours. If you keep a *positive, calm tone,* your child will have a harder time responding in a rude or defensive way. For example, a father and child recently had an experience that could have escalated, but thanks to the father's calm tone and the grandparents' intuition, the situation ended marvelously. A young girl was leaving a party with a blue balloon, which got away as she got out of the car. She was upset and crying. Instead of being angry at the girl for letting the balloon go or getting equally upset, Dad told her the balloon would travel to someone else's house as a gift from her. She brightened and smiled, saying, "Maybe it will even go to Gramma and Grampa's house!" The grandparents, who live far away, called the girl later to tell her they had just received a blue balloon. She was elated. Twice after this incident the child has voluntarily let go of balloons so they can make a trip to her grandparents' house.

Setting a positive tone is easier if you *use statements* rather than asking questions. Try to *state your intentions* without asking a question or making an accusation. For example, instead of saying, *"You'd better put those clothes away, or else!"* or *"Can you put those clothes away?"* try making a calm statement: *"Please put those clothes away in the next 10 minutes, and then you can go outside and play."*

Here are some more examples of how parents can state requests calmly so the child hears you. We also give you a chance to practice.

Child's Disruptive Behavior	Parent's Positive Tone
Your son returns the car to you with an almost empty gas tank.	"I want the gas tank to be filled when you use the car. If not, then you may not borrow it the next day."
Your daughter returns home one hour later than her agreed-on curfew, claiming she "forgot."	"I understand friends are important, but you are late. You will not be allowed to go out on Friday evening."

NOW YOU TRY IT:

My Child's Disruptive Behavior

1. _____

2. _____

How I Listened and Responded

1. _____

2. _____

Step 3. Give alternatives.

Sometimes *children get stuck* and don't stop and think before they act. Help your child develop better ways to deal with being angry or frustrated by offering alternative solutions to problems and other ways to express anger and frustration. You will learn specific behavioral plans and solutions later in this book, but you probably already have some good ideas.

Here are some examples of parents who gave their children other ideas and ways to handle frustration more appropriately.

Child's Angry Behavior	**Parent's New Solution**
After Julie's sister destroyed her makeup, Julie is found smacking her sister's arm and kicking her.	"I understand you're angry, but hitting is not allowed. Come to the other room and we'll figure this out together." (Julie is guided to walk away and talk, rather than to hit when angry.)
When you ask your son to join a family outing, he screams, "NO WAY!" and runs to his room.	"I'm here to listen to your reasons for not joining us, but please talk instead of yell, so I can hear you better."

NOW YOU TRY IT:

Child's Angry Behavior

1. _____

2. _____

Parent's New Solution

1. _____

2. _____

Step 4. Provide rewards, consequences, and negotiation.

As a parent you can "shape" your child's behavior in three important ways:

- Providing rewards like praise, attention, hugs, and tangibles.

- Setting firm, fair, and consistent limits like grounding, time-out, and taking away privileges.

- Negotiating and compromising (give and take).

When your child is having a hard time, and is angry or upset, sometimes a more structured intervention is called for.

Though we will review this in detail later, let's talk a bit about rewards first. Always reward your child more than you punish. Here's our golden rule. It is called the ***Three-to-One Principle.*** Parents must notice and reward *three* good behaviors for every *one* behavior that is punished. It is important to reward your child's self-controlled behavior and notice your child behaving well. Not only will your child adore this attention and likely repeat the good behavior, but you will feel better too. Rewards don't have to be material things like toys, prizes, stickers, and money. Your attention alone is sometimes enough. Give a hug, say something comforting, praise, praise, praise!

Please write down several rewards that your child would enjoy. (We suggest that you confer with your child first.)

1. _____

2. _____

3. _____

4. _____

5. _____

6. _____

When limits have to be set—and they will have to be sooner or later—remember to be persistent and consistent—*follow through with what you say.* Always offer a punishment that you can live with, that is reasonable, that "fits the crime," and that you feel is fair. Ask yourself: *"Am I really going to go through with that?" "How much will that punishment disrupt my day?" "How likely is it that this punishment will really work?"*

Parents can also use what we call *"natural and logical consequences"* that are age-appropriate. Natural consequences are just that—things that happen naturally but that feel punitive to a child. For example, you ask your child twice to wear a hat to school because it's a bit brisk and cold out. Your child refuses to wear a hat. The natural consequence is that he is uncomfortably cold on his way to school. Tomorrow he will probably choose to wear a hat!

Ignoring a situation is easy to do but hard to remember to do. Children yearn for our attention, and you have been reading about choosing your battles. Sometimes the best solution is no solution at all. Turning your head away, putting on earplugs, listening to a Walkman, and singing to yourself are some ways you can use to take your attention away. Obviously, you would not do this in any kind of dangerous situation, but the next time your two children are arguing over a TV show, see what happens if you ignore their desires to get you involved. They might just learn to agree on their own, thereby practicing social skills and leaving you out of the whole thing.

Finally, it is important to be able to negotiate and compromise with your children. Is there a solution to a problem that makes you both happy? Agreements that are clear and made ahead of time can truly help your child stay calm and in control. If your child agrees to something ahead of time, he/she is more likely to stick with it when it comes up.

Please read the following examples, and then try it yourself:

Child's Behavior	Parent's Response
Against his will, he joins the family for dinner rather than go out with friends.	"I'm so excited that you're here! Tell us about your afternoon at the park." (Parent offers verbal praise.)
Even though she's in an irritable mood, she gets off the couch to complete a chore.	"I really appreciate your helping out around here. Let me give you a hug along with your weekly allowance." (Parent offers physical affection and monetary reward.)
Your daughter is nagging you to drive her to the mall right away.	You ignore the nagging, and say, "*First* pick up the things you left in the den, ask me in a grown-up voice, and *then* I will be happy to drive you." (Parent offers a compromise.)

NOW YOU TRY IT:

My Child's Behavior

1. _____

2. _____

My Reward/Consequence/Negotiation

1. _____

2. _____

Let's sum up what we've covered here, because it is a lot. In order to help your child stay calm and in control, there are a few things you can do: Listen without offering advice or lecturing. Set a positive tone by remaining calm and using statements. Give alternative options. Provide lots of rewards, some consequences when necessary, and negotiation whenever possible.

Three Parenting Styles

A great deal of research has been done on "parenting styles," meaning the ways parents generally approach and interact with their children. The three most common parenting styles are Authoritarian, Permissive, and Authoritative. We'll describe them for you and let you decide which category describes you best.

Authoritarian—These parents have difficulty with their child because they are too strict and too rigid, and they value unquestioned obedience. They may be unaware of the child's need for some autonomy. Authoritarian parents discourage expressions of disagreement, may be more likely to use physical punishment, and rarely have reasoned discussions with their child. Children of these types of parents tend to be unsociable, unfriendly, and more withdrawn than other children their age.

An example of an authoritarian parent is a mother who, without discussion or negotiation, expects her 14-year-old daughter to remain at home every afternoon after school.

How often does this parenting style seem like you?
__very often   __sometimes   __rarely   __never

If you have some characteristics of an authoritarian parent, try to negotiate more often and see how your child can earn some privileges that allow for increased independence.

Permissive—These parents have difficulty with their child because they are too lenient and they provide inconsistent guidance and direction. Permissive parents, although warm, do not set firm and consistent limits. Children of these types of parents tend to be immature, moody, and dependent, and to have lower self-esteem than other children their age.

An example of a permissive parent is a father who allows his 9-year-old son to come home late from school without calling or providing an explanation.

How often does this parenting style seem like you?
    __very often   __sometimes   __rarely   __never

If you have characteristics of a permissive parent, try to be more involved in your child's life and learn to set firm, fair, and consistent limits. Praise your child for following new rules.

Authoritative—These parents are firm and they set clear limits for their children. As children get older, authoritative parents try to reason and explain things to them. They also set clear goals and encourage their children's independence. Children of these types of parents fare best—their social skills are strong and appropriate, and they are likeable, self-reliant, and cooperative.

An example of an authoritative parent is a mother of a 12-year-old boy who explains that he can't go to the movies with his friend on Friday evening because he neglected his school work three days in a row. But she tells him he can earn an outing with a friend next weekend if he does not neglect his homework.

How often does this parenting style seem like you?
    __very often   __sometimes   __rarely   __never

If you use an authoritative parenting style most of the time, congratulations and keep up the good parenting!

Before you read ahead, please go back to the beginning of this chapter and take time to practice ways of keeping your child calm. Fill in the spaces we have provided to write in examples of your own. Use these strategies the next time a conflict comes up in the family, and remember your parenting style.

Chapter 6

Communicating Effectively

There's talking, and then there's *communicating*. Often, parents come to us asking why what they are doing isn't working well enough. They tell us, "We argue about everything, and nothing ever gets resolved!"

Before we go on, please take this quiz:

Look over the following list of communication habits. Many of these habits may apply to you. Please check off ALL that apply to you. Think about your communication during the PAST WEEK.

CHECK IF YOU SOMETIMES DO THIS:	CHECK IF YOU DO THIS INSTEAD:
1. __ Call each other names	__ Express anger without hurt
2. __ Put each other down	__ Say "I'm angry that you did that"
3. __ Interrupt	__ Take turns talking; keep it short
4. __ Lecture; go on and on and on	__ Use no more than 10 words
5. __ Look away from the speaker	__ Use eye contact
6. __ Slouch	__ Sit up and look attentive
7. __ Get off the topic easily	__ Finish one topic, then go on

8. __	Think the worst, then get frantic	__	Focus on the positive and stay calm
9. __	Dredge up the past	__	Stick to the present
10. __	Read each other's mind	__	Ask each other's opinion
11. __	Command; order around	__	Request politely
12. __	Give the "silent treatment"	__	Talk about what's bothering you
13. __	Label the child as being "bad"	__	Label the behavior as being "bad"
14. __	Use an angry tone of voice	__	Use a pleasant, calm tone of voice
15. __	Start statements with "You"	__	Start statements with "I"

Now review your checklist. Communication habits on the left side are the "Don't's" and the common traps we all fall into now and again. Habits you checked off on the right side are the "Do's"— congratulations on using some of them!

Now you will be able to read about how to get rid of your Don't's and how to increase your Do's.

Remember what we said at the beginning of the chapter? That parents often ask why, if they are trying so hard, nothing seems to work. Generally, the problem is that parents are stuck in the ways they communicate with their family. You know that "weak" communication is occurring in your family if your desires are unclear to others, if messages are misconstrued, or if you aren't able to get your point across relatively quickly. Think about how often you say something you really don't mean or you feel a certain way about something but don't express that. These are examples of communication that is weak or lacking. On the other hand, your family is using "strong" communication if ideas are easily understood, if you feel validated after you say something, and if what you say matches up with how you act and how you feel.

Let's review this a little more clearly. In this chapter we will address a set of *listening and speaking skills*. These skills can be strengthened in your family to facilitate more effective communication and therefore better relationships. Here are some Do's and Don't's for listening and for speaking with others.

DO'S AND DON'T'S OF COMMUNICATION

LISTENING SKILLS

Remember: Listening in and of itself can help resolve some children's behavior problems.

Do's for Listening:

✓ Show interest, give the speaker your full attention, and stay alert.

✓ Remain *calm* no matter what you hear.

✓ Use reflective listening—that is, *say back what you hear.*

✓ Be open-minded and willing to change your ideas. Try to learn something from the speaker.

✓ Validate feelings of the speaker ("You're telling me that you're sad, right?").

✓ Use *eye contact* and other appropriate *nonverbal behavior.* This includes nodding your head and sitting up straight.

✓ Use open-ended questions to get more information about what you are hearing. For example, start by asking "How...?," "When...?," or "Why...?"

✓ Remember, the speaker is someone you care about—not an enemy. Your goal is to learn how to get along peacefully.

✓ Remain neutral. You don't have to agree to disagree with the speaker. Just try to listen and understand his/her point of view.

Don't's for Listening:

✗ Don't interrupt or get defensive. An excellent way to practice this is to count silently to five with a calm look on your face before you say anything.

✗ Don't give advice unless you are asked for it.

✗ Don't change the topic.

✗ Don't listen to anyone who is too upset and rude to talk to you.

✗ Don't add your own thoughts or feelings unless you are asked to.

✗   Don't listen to your child if he/she is too upset to talk. Wait until he/she is calm.

SPEAKING SKILLS

As we said in the previous chapter about "setting a positive tone," the way something is said affects the listener's response. For example, if you use an *angry tone*, the listener gets defensive, and this may cause an argument. On the other hand, if you use a *calm tone*, the child won't be so defensive, the situation may be diffused, and the discussion can go on.

Do's for Speaking:

✓   Wait for an opportune moment to speak (you're calm, the child's calm).

✓   Be aware of your tone of voice.

✓   Use "I" messages. Begin sentences saying "I feel...," "I think...," or "I believe...."

✓   Be brief and specific. Use *no more than 10 words*, and make your point only twice.

✓   Make statements rather than asking questions or making accusations.

✓   *State what you want, not what you don't want.* For example, instead of saying "I *don't* want your clothes on the floor" say "I *would like you to* pick up those clothes in the next 10 minutes, and then you can go outside."

Don't's for Speaking:

✗   Don't use back-handed comments or bring up the past. Here's an example of a back-handed comment: *"You did a nice job cleaning your room. Too bad you never do that— if you had done it that way last week, we wouldn't have had a fight about it!"*

✗   Don't label the child. Instead, label the behavior that you want to change.

✗ Don't nag, argue, or place blame on the listener.

✗ Don't bring up lots of problems at once; tackle one at a time.

✗ Don't lecture. Children stop hearing you after about 10 words anyway.

✗ Don't tease or use name-calling, even in jest.

✗ Don't hog the conversation by talking too much and not allowing the other person to have a chance to say something. It's hard to pay attention to someone who goes on and on and on and on...right?

Of all the Do's and Don't's, the most important one is to *know how to translate your questions and accusations into statements.* In talking with children, and especially teenagers, parents often ask way too many questions and make assumptions. This tends to put children on the defensive, and it may encourage lying.

Below is an exercise that focuses on how to translate questions into statements using the phrases *"I'd like...," "I want...," and "I expect...."* By making changes in what you say, you not only minimize power struggles but also begin to set clearer expectations in a respectful way. Changing how you say something may make it easier for your child to listen to you.

Helpful Hints

✓ Minimize blame by starting with the word "I" rather than "You."

✓ Avoid cornering your child by making statements rather than asking questions.

✓ Be sure your expectations are clear—be specific about what you want.

✓ Be sure to choose the word that best expresses *how strong* your feelings are about an issue. "I wish..." is not as strong as "I expect...," so think ahead about how you phrase what you say.

Here are some examples.

Old Statement:	"Where is my blouse you borrowed?"
New Statement:	"I would like my blouse to be returned in clean condition by tomorrow, or I will not lend you clothes to wear this weekend."
Old Statement:	"You'd better call me at work before you leave the house, or else, young man!"
New Statement:	"I expect a phone call at work before you leave the house, so that I know what your plans are."

NOW YOU TRY IT:

Old Statement:	*"Why don't you come home a bit earlier tonight so that you aren't so tired in the morning?"*
New Statement:	

_____

Old Statement:	*"Don't you dare use that kind of language with me!"*
New Statement:	

_____

Old Statement:	*"You always ask for money first, and then you never do any chores."*
New Statement:	

_____

Now we've reviewed effective skills for listening and speaking. Without explaining to your family that you are doing something new, practice using **active listening** once each day during the next week. This includes looking at the speaker, paraphrasing what is being said, nodding your head, staying calm, and responding appropriately. Use the Do's and Don't's listed in this chapter to guide you.

Remember the checklist you completed at the beginning of this chapter? Here it is again, but now you have learned something new. **ONE WEEK after you read and practice skillful communication, please fill out this checklist again. Look over the following list of communication habits. Many of these habits may apply to you. Please check off ALL that apply to you. Think about the PAST ONE WEEK:**

CHECK IF YOU SOMETIMES DO THIS:	**CHECK IF YOU DO THIS INSTEAD:**
1. __ Call each other names	__ Express anger without hurt
2. __ Put each other down	__ Say "I'm angry that you did that"
3. __ Interrupt	__ Take turns talking; keep it short
4. __ Lecture; go on and on and on	__ Use no more than 10 words
5. __ Look away from the speaker	__ Use eye contact
6. __ Slouch	__ Sit up and look attentive
7. __ Get off the topic easily	__ Finish one topic, then go on
8. __ Think the worst, then get frantic	__ Focus on the positive and stay calm
9. __ Dredge up the past	__ Stick to the present
10. __ Read each other's mind	__ Ask each other's opinion
11. __ Command; order around	__ Request politely
12. __ Give the "silent treatment"	__ Talk about what's bothering you
13. __ Label the child as being "bad"	__ Label the behavior as being "bad"
14. __ Use an angry tone of voice	__ Use a pleasant, calm tone of voice
15. __ Start statements with "You"	__ Start statements with "I"

Look over your checklist. How is it different from the one you filled out at the beginning of this chapter?

My communication habits that have improved this week include:

a. _____

b. _____

c. _____

The areas where I still need to practice communication skills include:

a. _____

b. _____

c. _____

CLUES

Before you go on, we wanted to give you some **helpful hints** about turning your questions and accusations into statements. Here are some ways to answer the section above.

Old Statement:	*"Why don't you come home a bit earlier tonight so that you aren't so tired in the morning?"*
New Statement:	*"I would like you home a little earlier tonight so that you aren't so tired in the morning."*
Old Statement:	*"Don't you dare use that kind of language with me!"*
New Statement:	*"I expect you to use appropriate language when we talk."*
Old Statement:	*"You always ask for money first, and then you never do any chores."*

New Statement: *"I feel confused, because sometimes I pay you allowance but the chores don't get done right away."*

CHAPTER 7

Problem-Solving Effectively

You have now learned a bit about managing your own frustration and helping your child remain calm and not get out of control. You have also learned the importance of working together and communicating effectively.

So now let's turn to one of the biggest obstacles in parenting—how to solve problems effectively and without much disruption to your family. Problems can be fairly easy to resolve most of the time if you think about several important steps in advance. These are eight important steps.

1. Specify what the problem is.

2. Think about everyone's perspective on the problem.

3. Generate as many possible solutions as you can.

4. Select one of these solutions.

5. Use the solution when the problem occurs.

6. Assess the effectiveness of the solution.

7. Monitor the problem over time.

8. Try other solutions if the problem persists.

Step 1. Specify what the problem is.

One reason parents have difficulty making changes is that they forget to break problems down into specific concrete issues. Instead, they over-whelm themselves by trying to tackle a situation that is too vague.

The first step to problem-solving is to *think of one specific problem you want solved.* The best way to do this is to think about our helpful hints.

Helpful Hints

✓ Can you think of only one problem at a time?

✓ Is the problem simple and concrete? You should be able to describe the problem in one or two brief sentences. For example, *"he's rude"* is too vague, but *"she doesn't get up for school at 7:20"* is simple and concrete.

✓ Is the problem something you can see or observe? It's important to focus on problems that you have some control over, like a behavior at home or in the neighborhood, rather than something that occurs on the playground.

✓ Is the problem something you can visualize in your mind? If you told friends about the problem, could they get a clear picture of it from your description?

✓ Does the problem describe a particular *behavior* rather than a general attitude or characteristic of your child? Describe what the child is doing or saying.

Step 1—Example

One specific, concrete problem about a child refusing to go to bed at the agreed-upon time would be: *"My daughter agreed that her bedtime would be 9:00 on school nights. However, most nights she gets out of bed or asks for a drink until at least one hour past her bedtime."*

Can you see how this example illustrates the hints above? We've kept the problem focused on one issue, we can visualize it, it is observable to others, and it pertains to a behavior rather than an attitude or characteristic of the child.

NOW YOU TRY IT:

What is one problem you want solved?

_____

_____

Step 2. Think about everyone's perspective on the problem.

Before parents solve any problems in their family, it is important for them to see their own point of view as well as the child's.

The second step to problem-solving, then, is to *think about how you and your child might view the situation in a different way.* Here are more helpful hints.

Helpful Hints

✓ Can you put yourself in another family member's shoes? What would they say about the problem? Would the other person be as concerned about the problem as you are?

✓ How would you want the problem resolved, and how would the other person involved in the problem want it resolved?

Step 2—Example

Perspective-taking means that you consider your view and that of your child. Perspective on your child refusing to go to bed at the agreed-upon time would be as follows:

PARENT'S VIEW: *"I worry that my daughter will be too tired to get up for school." Or, "I need this time for myself to get chores done and pay bills, so my daughter should be in bed at 9:00."*

CHILD'S VIEW: *"My daughter thinks it is no big deal to be up late, is not worried about being tired in the morning, has a favorite TV show on at 9:15, and doesn't realize that I have things I need to do once she goes to bed."*

Can you see how this example illustrates the hints above? The parent and child perspectives were clearly described and well thought out.

NOW YOU TRY IT:

Parent's view of the problem is.

_____

Child's view of the problem is.

_____

Step 3. Generate as many possible solutions as you can.

Parents often get stuck solving problems because they go with their first inclination—they pick the *first* thing they think of to solve a problem. Instead, if parents have a list of possible solutions, they can make an informed decision ahead of time about the "best" solution to a problem.

The third step to problem-solving is to *generate a list of as many possible solutions as you can.* We have provided a list of some Problem-Solving Solutions following step 8 below. Please review them carefully. Again, here are helpful hints:

Helpful Hints

✓   How creative and free can you be? Anything goes, so list as many ideas as you can.

✓   Can you list ideas without judging them? We are so hard on ourselves sometimes, but here it is important to list ideas without saying whether they are strong or weak ideas, or whether they would work or not. That comes later.

✓   What solutions can come from skills you've learned in previous chapters? How about listening, or setting a positive tone, or providing a reward or consequence?

✓   Is a trade-off possible? Remember to use oral or written contracts.

✓ Have you carefully reviewed the Problem-Solving Solutions that follow step 8?

Step 3—Example
Some creative solutions to our problem about a child refusing to go to bed at the agreed-upon time would be:

Take privileges away for going to bed late.
Reward my daughter for going to bed on time.
Scream at her.
Ignore her going to bed late.
Negotiate a plan or a contract.
Give her more chores to do.
Ground her for life.

Can you see how this example illustrates the hints above? We've come up with seven potential ideas, and we were creative about our solutions without saying whether they were strong or weak or whether they would work well or not.

NOW YOU TRY IT:
Without censoring your ideas, list as many possible solutions as you can. Feel free to use the Problem-Solving Solutions listed after step 8 for other ideas.

_____

_____

_____

_____

_____

_____

_____

Before we move on, we'd like to acknowledge that this step-by-step process must seem long and arduous to you by now. It probably even seems like overkill, and you may feel it would be easier just to put the book away. It is hard work at first, but if you follow this process once or twice it will become easier, and then you'll see how effective you can become at solving problems with your children.

Step 4. Select one of these solutions.

Once you've come up with lots of possibilities, it is time to select one thing to try. Do you see how this step-by-step process prepares you to make informed decisions about solving problems?

The fourth step is to *decide on one solution you would like to try.* Here are some more helpful hints.

Helpful Hints

✓ What are the positive and negative aspects of each idea you came up with?

✓ Which solution would solve the problem most quickly?

✓ Which idea is the least conflictual? Think about what would not disrupt your family life as much.

✓ Will this idea really work? Can you live with this solution?

Step 4—Example

One strong solution to solving the problem of a child refusing to go to bed at the agreed-upon time would be: *"We will reward her for going to bed on time."*

This solution is more likely to work than, say, screaming at the child (which we'd never advocate doing); grounding her for life (which is ridiculous, unreasonable, and impossible to carry out); or ignoring the problem (which might make it worse). There were other strong solutions, like taking away privileges. But rewarding positive behavior is almost always more effective than punishing negative behavior. The reason we didn't decide to negotiate a plan is that the bedtime was already agreed on and she had difficulty adhering to the negotiated bedtime.

NOW YOU TRY IT:

What is the best of all of your ideas?

_____

The pros and cons of my other ideas are

_____

_____

_____

_____

_____

Step 5. Use the solution when the problem occurs.

Once you've selected a solution to try, it is time to try it. When the problem occurs, think about what you will do to solve it.

The fifth step is to *put your idea into action when the problem occurs.* Here are some more helpful hints.

Helpful Hints

✓ Are you calm first, before you try the solution?

✓ Are you in control of your emotions?

✓ Are you able to try to solution right away, in the moment that the problem occurs? It is almost always best to solve a problem immediately.

Step 5—Example

The solution chosen was to create a reward system for the bedtime problem. Here's an example of what parents might come up with: "If our daughter goes to bed within 10 minutes of her 9:00 p.m. bedtime, we will reward her with a special treat or activity of her choice the next day. The rewards will include a favorite dessert after dinner, a prize worth up to 50 cents, spending some uninterrupted time with Mom, or some brief time on the computer (her favorite hobby, usually permitted only on weekends)."

As we have mentioned, most children are motivated by external rewards, which parents can fade out over time as the problem behavior diminishes. However, keep in mind that contracts such as this one are very child-specific—what is rewarding to one child may be a punishment to another! A discussion with your child about likes, dislikes, and potential rewards can go a long way to make a contract work well.

NOW YOU TRY IT:

What we will do is

_____

The reason this is likely to work is

_____

_____

_____

Step 6. Assess the effectiveness of the solution.

Now you've tried one of your ideas. Well...how did it go?

The sixth step involves *evaluating the problem and figuring out if your solution worked.* In case you think we forgot about the helpful hints, here they are:

Helpful Hints

✓   Did you try your solution twice? Always give it not one but TWO chances to work before you consider that it won't work, or before you give up on it.

✓   Did the solution solve the problem quickly?

✓   Did the solution solve all of the problem or only part of it? For example, the child in our example might be in her room at 9:00

but not in her bed trying to fall asleep. This would be only a partial success.

Step 6—Example

The reward system was explained to the child, and rewards/privileges were agreed on. Here's what happened: *"The first night we spent a lot of time talking about the plan and she was excited to get ice cream after dinner, so she got in bed at about 9:05. Although she asked once for water, she was asleep in about 15 minutes. The next evening she was amply rewarded with a large scoop of chocolate chip on a cone. However, the next night we had a problem—she wanted to stay up later because her favorite TV show was on. With all the fuss, she ended up going to bed late, but the next day she expected a reward anyway. Of course, she was not granted a reward. But we reminded her about the plan again. We almost gave up, thinking that rewards maybe weren't such a good idea, but we tried the third night and, lo and behold, she was in bed on time."*

NOW YOU TRY IT:

The solution was/was not (circle one) successful and here's what happened:

_____

_____

_____

Step 7: Monitor the problem over time.

Now you've tried one of your solutions to a problem at least twice. Even if it works initially, it may or may not work over time. A strong solution is one that remains relatively effective over several weeks or months, even if you adapt and modify it. Your children will never be "perfect," but a strong solution to a problem is one that could basically become part of your everyday routine.

The seventh step, then, involves monitoring the problem over time. Again, here are some helpful hints to consider.

Helpful Hints
- ✓ Have you noticed the problem occurring often enough to interrupt your daily life?
- ✓ Have you been tracking changes after you try the solution at least twice?
- ✓ Has implementing the solution become easier or a part of your everyday life?

Step 7—Example:
The reward system seemed to work over time. Here's what has been happening in the past six weeks: *"We noticed that the first few weeks were relatively successful. Every now and then we have a problem with bedtime and she knows she won't get her reward the next day. At this point the 9:00 bedtime has become such a routine that our daughter really doesn't mind it. Rather than rewarding her with tangible things, we now give her lots of praise and encouragement and our attention before bedtime. This really gets her motivated. And sometimes, when she's really had a good day, we surprise her with a special privilege and mention how much we appreciate having a peaceful evening before bedtime."*

NOW YOU TRY IT:
After a reasonable amount of time has passed—at least a few weeks—come back to this page and fill out the following information about the problem:

The problem has/has not (circle one) continued and here's what has been happening:

_____

_____

_____

Step 8. Try other solutions if the problem persists.

If the problem you were tackling is solved, GOOD WORK! What you tried worked, and you should be proud of yourself. Now you can go back to step 1 to work on another specific problem you might be having.

If the problem is not fully solved, or if the solution you tried didn't work for some reason, *return to step 4 to decide on another idea.* Here are some helpful hints.

Helpful Hints

✓ Why do you think the solution you selected didn't work effectively?

✓ How can you pick a stronger idea from your list?

✓ Do you need to generate more ideas in step 4 before you move on?

Step 8—Example

Here's what happened: *"The reward system worked over time and we have been pleased with the results. Now we want to deal with our son's tantrums whenever we take him to the supermarket. We'll have to go to step 1 and follow this process along the way."*

NOW YOU TRY IT:

Was the problem solved, or did you have to go back to step 4 and try other ideas?

Here's what happened:

_____

_____

_____

Problem-Solving Solutions

In this section we list several kinds of problem-solving solutions, followed by samples of some of them.

Contracts

✓ Grandma's Rule ("First..., then...") is an oral contract. For example, "first straighten up your room, then you can play your video games." Or *"first keep your hands and feet to yourself on the playground, then we can go buy our ice cream cone."*

✐ The other kind of contract is a written contract, in which you and your child negotiate a plan together and then sign your names to show that you both agree. (Sample A. Parent-Child Contract)

Rewards

☺ Positive attention is a powerful reward for children, even though it takes a lot of effort sometimes. Provide your child with praise, loving gestures, private conversations, or doing something special together. Do you remember the Three-to-One Principle mentioned in chapter 5? What this principle means is that you must notice and reward three good behaviors for every one behavior that you punish. (Sample B. ABCs for Building Children's Self-Esteem; Sample C. The Language of Encouragement; Sample D. 10 Strategies for Encouraging Teens)

★ Point charts help increase positive behavior by giving a child the chance to earn points or star stickers, which are then exchanged for rewards. Rewards can vary greatly from child to child, but they might include a small toy, going to a party, renting a video, or a nominal amount of money. (Sample E. Point-Reward Calendar for Improving Several Behaviors) Also, go back to step 4 in chapter 5 for more information about the use of rewards.

Consequences

☹ Set firm, fair, and consistent limits that are age-appropriate. The punishment should fit the crime, and never be too punitive or extreme. As a parent you must be firm and clear, and always follow through with what you have told the child. Therefore, it is important to select a punishment that you can follow through with.

Here's an example of what can happen when you don't take the time to problem-solve effectively and then end up saying something you don't mean: We recently had parents who came to us complaining that their 14-year-old son was disobeying curfew. When asked what they did to try to solve this problem, they said, "We simply told him that the next time he came home late we'd throw his bed and clothing on the front lawn." These were clearly frustrated parents making an idle threat. The son said, "Of course, I'm gonna come home late— they'd never do that because they'd be embarrassed in front of the neighbors."

⊗ Time-out is an effective consequence for many young children. Okay...you're thinking that you've already tried this a hundred times and it never works, right? There are ways to use time-out effectively. (Sample F. Using Time-Out Effectively.)

⇥ Use natural and logical consequences whenever possible. What this means is that you can sometimes take advantage of punishments that will simply occur on their own. For example, if a child breaks his sibling's toy on purpose, he has to use his weekly allowance to replace it. If a child refuses to wear a winter hat in the morning, his ears will be freezing by the time he gets to school. This is a natural consequence of not wearing a hat, and it will probably be powerful enough to get the child to put a hat on the next day.

✗ Ignore negative behavior if the behavior is more a minor infraction than a dangerous or serious problem. Here are some ways of ignoring negative behavior: refuse to scold, argue, or talk to your child while he/she is exhibiting the behavior; turn your head or walk away without showing your own anger or frustration in your manner or gestures; or act absorbed in some other activity. Always remember to give your child a lot of attention when the negative behavior stops, and reward good alternative behavior.

Co-parenting
☺ ● Working as a "parenting team" with your spouse or partner or best friend or relative makes parenting less stressful, more enjoyable, and easier. Children need to see their parents working together and collaborating. Please go back to chapter 3 for further details.

Modeling
☛ Set a good example for your child. This is a powerful tool, because children learn from observing others.

Parents came into our office complaining that their 10-year-old son Matthew cursed at the son of friends of theirs when the two families were at a barbeque together. Matthew's father reprimanded and punished Matthew on the spot for using such terrible language. Matthew looked at his father in a confused way and said, "But Daddy, you say it all the time!" Matthew's parents could not have been more embarrassed, and it occurred to them that children really are impressionable.

Effective Instructions

☛ A final factor in solving problems effectively is learning to be effective in instructing your child on what behavior you want to stop or change. A command is a request to immediately start or stop a behavior. All parents must be able to give clear, effective instructions and commands on occasion. They must also be able to back up their commands.

When are commands given? Give your child a command when your want him/her to *stop* a specific *misbehavior* and you believe that he/she might disobey a simple request to stop the misbehavior. Also, give a command when you want your child to *start* a particular behavior and you believe your child might disobey a simple request to start the behavior.

How should you give a command? Follow the guidelines listed below.

GIVING EFFECTIVE COMMANDS TO YOUR CHILD—PARENT'S CHECKLIST

Steps to Follow

1. Move close to your child.
2. Have a stern facial expression.
3. Say his or her name.
4. Get and maintain eye contact.
5. Use a firm tone of voice.
6. Give a direct, simple, and clear command.

   ✓ Use no more than 10 words.

   ✓ Say what you want, not what you don't want.

   ✓ Make a statement, rather than ask a question.

7. Back up your command if necessary, with a consequence or a reward.

Chapter 7 Samples

Sample A. Parent-Child Contract

I, _____
  (child's name)

agree to: _____

_____

_____

I, _____
  (parent's name)

agree to: _____

_____

_____

Date contract begins: _____

Date contract ends: _____

Date contract signed: _____

Agreed to by:

_____
           (child's signature)

_____
           (parent's signature)

Sample B. ABCs for Building Children's Self-Esteem

Accept and acknowledge them just as they are.

Be there to see them perform.

Celebrate their birthdays and special events.

Develop a routine for study time.

Encourage them to achieve their best.

Find their assets and guide them to build on them.

Give a gift for no special reason.

Help them do things.

Influence them through mutual respect and a cohesive relationship.

Join them for trips to the store, ball games, and other activities.

Know where they are, what they are doing, and with whom they are doing it.

Listen with interest and empathy.

Model the behavior you want from them.

Nurture them according to their needs, not necessarily their desires.

Omit criticism and complaining after a failure or disappointment.

Provide the tools and materials for achievement.

Question them about their friends and the parents of their friends.

Respect their privacy.

Smile unless you are angry or correcting them.

Touch them every time you can, especially when you tell them you trust them.

Unite them to a cause greater than themselves.

Visit their teacher at least two times a year.

Welcome their friends in your home.

Xercise with the children.

Yearn for their happiness.

Zero in on their strengths for career development.

Sample C. The Language of Encouragement

1. I like the way you handled that.

2. How do you feel about this?

3. I'm glad you enjoyed yourself.

4. Since you're not satisfied, what do you think you can do so you will be pleased with it?

5. You'll make it!

6. You're making progress.

7. I believe you'll handle it.

8. I have confidence in your judgment.

9. I can see you put a lot of effort into that.

10. I can see a lot of progress.

11. You're improving in _____ (say something specific).

12. Looks like you're moving along.

13. You may not feel that you've reached your goal, but look how far you've come.

14. Thanks for helping—it took a load off me.

15. You have a talent for _____ (say something specific).

16. Would you help me with this?

17. I really appreciate your help on _____.

Sample D. 10 Strategies for Encouraging Teens

1. Give responsibility.

2. Show appreciation for things done at home.

3. Ask your teen for opinions and suggestions.

4. Encourage participation in decision making.

5. Accept mistakes.

6. Emphasize the process, not just the product.

7. Turn liabilities into assets.

8. Show confidence in your teen's judgment.

9. Have positive expectations.

10. Develop alternative ways of viewing situations.

Sample E. Point-Reward Calendar for Improving Several Behaviors

Points Earned

List of good behaviors and possible points	Sun	Mon	Tues	Wed	Thur	Fri	Sat
Total Points Earned							

This calendar provides a record of several behaviors for one week. Post a new calendar for each week.

At the end of each day, total the number of points your child has earned. Draw marks through points on the bottom line when your child "spends" those points.

Helpful Hints

✓ Decide *when* to give rewards (each day, at the end of each week, the first day of each month, etc.).

✓ Think about your *child's age* (younger children require immediate rewards; older children can wait for weekly or monthly rewards that they save up points for).

✓ Use *tangible rewards* at the beginning (like a prize, toy, or money).

✓ Gradually replace tangible rewards with *social rewards* (like praise, hugs, a note, or a special time together).

✓ Always *follow through* with what you agree to with your child.

Sample F. Using Time-Out Effectively

✔ **Steps to Follow**

_____1. Select one target behavior to use time-out to correct.

_____2. Count how often this behavior occurs, so you know if it is getting better.

_____3. Pick out a boring place for time-out.

_____4. Explain time-out to your child.

_____5. Wait for the target behavior to occur.

THE TARGET BEHAVIOR OCCURS.

_____6. Place your child in the time-out place and use no more than 10 words and 10 seconds to do it.

_____7. Get a portable timer, and set it to ring in ____ minutes (1 minute for each year of the child's age). Place it within hearing distance of the child.

_____8. Wait for the timer to ring. Do not give your child any kind of attention until the timer rings.

_____9. After the timer rings, ask your child why he/she was sent to time-out, and talk about ways to help the child behave better next time.

REMEMBER:

✓ Get your child's attention by using a stern facial expression and saying his/her name.

✓ Give direct, simple, and clear commands to get a child to time-out.

✓ Do not argue with your child before, during, or after time-out. Keep your attention away and use it as a reward for when your child is behaving.

✓ Do not use the bedroom, a rocking chair, or a comfortable couch for time-out. Find a boring place.

✓ Keep track of time yourself, or use the timer on the kitchen stove.

✓ Do not make the child apologize or promise to be "good" after leaving time-out. The punishment of time-out is enough.

✓ Do not try to shame or frighten your child with time-out.

Chapter 8

Enhancing Positive Behavior

By now you have learned a number of different skills to deal with your children's negative, problem behavior—skills like remaining calm, co-parenting, setting rewards and consequences, and effective communication and problem-solving. At this point your child's behavior should be under better control, and you should feel more competent in your ability to problem-solve and parent effectively. So far, you and your children have been working on the process of changing the environment to prevent problems and on learning communication and problem-solving skills.

The next stage is to develop *positive* parent-child interactions. We call these *"prosocial"* behaviors, and we now want you to focus on increasing *prosocial* or *positive behaviors* in your children. This stage includes focusing on their strengths and on building a more positive transactional relationship between parents and children. Here are examples of prosocial (positive) behavior: generosity, respect, responsibility, following through with requests, making new friends, keeping friends, joining a group activity, sharing, and making conversation.

When your child is having behavior problems, we know that it is difficult to shift your focus to positive behaviors or to what your child is doing well. But it is very important to facilitate prosocial and positive behavior even while you're dealing with behaviors that you don't like. The reason is that prosocial skills protect children from developing more severe problems and help them get along better with parents, other adults, and peers.

Sometimes beginning to notice and enhance positive things your child does can make parents nervous or uncomfortable. For example, parents may be afraid to leave behind their old familiar patterns, or afraid that they are giving in, or fearful that their children will take advantage of them.

Can you think of any fears you have about noticing and enhancing positive things your child does? If so, write them down in the space provided.

1. _____

2. _____

During this shift to the positive, parents may slip up or things may not work out as planned, and this is expected—parents will have minor setbacks. This is okay, but it is important to continue to make the effort to use new skills without getting discouraged. Take a few minutes to think about what will happen when you begin to shift your focus to your children's positive or prosocial behavior. For example, some parents expect that it might be difficult to start noticing good things that their children do.

What do you anticipate?

1. _____

2. _____

We have already mentioned some examples of prosocial behaviors.

What prosocial behaviors would you like to see in your child?

1. _____

2. _____

3. _____

Now we will review some simple techniques that can help you enhance your child's prosocial behavior.

1. Spend special, quality time with your child.

Most parents think of special time as something they do with younger children, but it can also be a very valuable pursuit for you and your pre-teen or teenager. You're probably thinking, "You must be kidding! My teen wants to spend time with me about as often as it rains in the desert."

Younger children have regular times with parents, like playing games or reading stories. Those meaningful moments can be comforting to teenagers who are struggling with giving up childhood. Most teens are very active, and adult life is rarely leisurely. If you never had special time with your child, this would be a great time to start. Special time gives you a chance to keep in touch with your growing teenager. One way to develop a better relationship is to suggest that you do something together once a month. Here are some suggestions that you could follow with your child or teenager.

- ✓ Spend one-on-one uninterrupted time with your child once a month. No phone calls, sibling rivalry, or household chores to spoil the fun. Don't use the time to talk about your child's problems unless he/she brings the subject up.

- ✓ Choose an activity you both enjoy, so you don't end up resenting it. Focus on mutually enjoyable activities like dinner, a movie, a sporting event, or a cultural performance.

- ✓ For teenagers: Even if your teenager does not respond well to your suggestion, try not to take it as a personal rejection. Your child may feel ambivalent or may be suspicious of your real intentions (for example, the teenager may think this is just a way for you to get a chance to deliver a lecture). Just say, *"We're all really busy, but I miss having time with you. I really would like it if we could do something special once a month. Please think about it— it could be fun. It's okay if you're not sure right now. We can talk about it again."*

✓ If your teenager rejects the idea, let him/her know it's okay and you still love him/her. This says to your teen that you accept his/her right to not spend time with you right now. It just means that he/she is growing up.

2. Tune in to desirable behavior.

This involves catching your child doing the right thing and positively attending to it. It is important to attend selectively. Some parents attend most often when their child is misbehaving. Often by attending to your child's negative behaviors you are inadvertently reinforcing the behavior you would like to get rid of. Instead, *catch your child being good* in order to increase the positives rather than the negatives. For example:

✓ Identify what you want your child to do more often.

✓ Praise your child enthusiastically by describing the behavior. For example, *"That's terrific, Andy. You came home before dinner tonight."* Be sincere, and don't mention past performance in reference to current success. For example, never say *"You did a good job, but...."*

✓ Attend to it *immediately* and often.

✓ Take an interest in what your child is doing. Your attention is a powerful motivator.

✓ Positive attention can include nonverbal behavior—sitting or standing nearby, touching a shoulder, smiling, or joining your child's activity.

✓ Use "I" statements to convey positive feelings. For example, *"I am so pleased you cleaned your room."*

✓ Attend to small improvements.

3. Give plenty of physical affection.

How family members touch is important. Positive affection involves physical contact such as touching, hugging, tickling, kissing, patting, and cuddling (depending on your child's age).

For example, you could:

✓ Vary your contact with your child.

✓ Avoid being rough.

✓ Avoid giving physical contact when your child is agitated and disruptive, to calm the child down.

✓ Combine touch with caring words. Tell your child you care.

Do not force physical contact.

4. Talk with your child.

This involves having brief conversations with your children about an activity or interest of theirs. You could try the following:

✓ Make interested comments such as *"You've nearly finished that book."* If the child responds, continue the conversation by making further comments.

✓ It helps to use open-ended questions. Begin with the words how, why, when, and where.

5. Provide engaging activities for children.

Sometimes it helps if parents set up situations to promote positive relationships and interactions. For example, you might arrange your child's physical and social environments with people you trust and admire, or provide age-appropriate activities with well-behaved peers. This creates and maintains opportunities for your child to develop social skills, be responsible, and feel good.

Also, you could suggest to your child that he/she start a *special project* that would involve doing something positive. Discuss some possibilities. You can use this list to give children ideas or have them come up with their own idea, such as

Do volunteer work.

Play a sport or coach a younger team.

Take music lessons.

Get a part-time job.

Tutor a younger child or peers after school.

Keep a daily diary.

Do an art project.

Be a class pet monitor.

Write an autobiography.

Spend time with an elderly person.

You may want to discuss a special project with your child and then complete the following plan together.

1. What I will do for my special project is:

1. _____

2. _____

2. The things I need to do to begin my project are:

1. _____

2. _____

3. _____

4. _____

3. It will take me _____ **(time frame) to complete my project.**

4. When my project is completed, I will talk to my parents about it.
Now that we have discussed some of the techniques to enhance positive behavior, which techniques do you think you will try, and why?

1. _____

2. _____

3. _____

We hope that by now you agree about the importance of focusing on and enhancing your child's positive behaviors. Practicing this parenting skill can be enjoyable for you and your children, and it can help make your family life more enjoyable.

Chapter 9

Conclusion

We have covered a lot of information about skillful parenting. Sometimes it's hard to sort out what is most important. Here are the **Top 10 Parenting Tips** if you're in a pinch.

1. **Be patient.** Change can be slow. (chapter 1)

2. **Stay calm.** If you are already angry at your child, you waited too long to intervene. (chapter 2)

3. **Co-parent and make private time** for yourself and your spouse/partner. (chapter 3)

4. **Pick three problems as priorities.** Decide ahead of time what's really important. (chapter 4)

5. **Look for chances to praise and reward** good behavior. Remember the Three-to-One Principle. (chapter 5)

6. **Follow through** with rewards and consequences. (chapter 5)

7. **Use no more than 10 words.** Keep directions short and simple. (chapter 6)

8. **Say what you want,** not what you don't want. (chapter 6)

9. **Use a solution twice** before you try a new solution to a problem. (chapter 7)

10. **Spend special, quality time** with your child every day. (chapter 8)

✂ Tear out and keep this with you

Top 10 Parenting Tips	Skillful Parenting

Top 10 Parenting Tips

1. Be patient
2. Stay calm
3. Co-parent and make private time
4. Pick three problems as priorities
5. Look for chances to praise/reward
6. Follow through
7. Use no more than 10 words
8. Say what you want
9. Use a solution twice
10. Spend special time

Skillful Parenting

1. Keep yourself calm
2. Co-parent
3. Choose your battles
4. Keep your child calm
5. Communicate effectively
6. Problem-solve effectively
7. Enhance positive behavior

Skillful Parenting Challenge

Now let's try the Skillful Parenting Challenge. Below are some descriptions of challenging situations that parents face every day. Now that you've read this book, you may be able to resolve these challenges with courage and confidence. The scenarios focus on children of all ages and from all walks of life—these are real situations that parents have brought to our attention and that will probably sound familiar to you.

Directions for the Skillful Parenting Challenge

1. Read each scenario.

2. Write down your first thought about how to handle the situation.

3. Read the "helpful hints" provided below.

4. Compare your answer with our hints. Were you on target? Were you mostly there? Were you absolutely dazed and confused?

5. If dazed and confused, go back to that particular chapter to review the skills.

GOOD LUCK!

Challenge 1

You arrive home from work to find your son playing computer games with three other boys whom you don't know very well. He is supposed to be doing his homework. What would your response be to this situation?

Your response:

1. _____

2. _____

Helpful Hints

✓ Did you keep yourself calm by using calming self-talk? (chapter 2)

✓ Because ignoring is not appropriate in this situation, what other possible consequences could you implement? (chapter 7)

✓ Did you remember any of the communication "do's" when trying to resolve this challenge? (chapter 6)

Challenge 2

Your child borrowed her sister's rollerblades. Instead of bringing them indoors, she forgot and left them outside in the rain, where they got ruined. As a parent, what should you do, if anything?

Your response:

1. _____

2. _____

Helpful Hints

✓ Did you think of using a humorous exaggeration here? (chapter 5)

✓ How much of a priority is this problem? Remember to choose your battles wisely. (chapter 4)

✓ Two possible solutions would be to have the child pay for new rollerblades out of his or her allowance, or to take away the privilege of borrowing rollerblades for the next two weeks. Parents help repair the damaged rollerblades. (chapter 7)

Challenge 3

Your daughter just finished a science project. The dog ran in and knocked it over and parts of it came flying off. She started sobbing, stomping her feet, and whining. It seemed as though nothing would comfort her. What could you do?

Your response:

1. _____

2. _____

Helpful Hints

✓ First, what do you think about your daughter's behavior, and how does it make you feel? Remember that thoughts, feelings, and actions are all connected. (chapter 2)

✓ How could you work with your spouse/partner to come up with an alternative solution for your daughter to salvage this challenging situation? (chapters 3 and 5)

Challenge 4
Your child surprises you by having washed all the dishes in the kitchen sink. However, one of your favorite glasses was broken in the process. How do you handle this situation?

Your response:

1. _____

2. _____

Helpful Hints

✓ Given that this is not one of your "top battles," what would be a way to lighten up the situation using humor? (chapter 2)

✓ Would you reward your child for doing the dishes, set a consequence for breaking a glass, or both? (chapter 7)

✓ How can you encourage positive behavior in the future? (chapter 8)

Challenge 5

Your child does not telephone you to tell you where he is, and it is past the dinner hour when he was expected home. How should you respond to this challenging but typical problem?

Your response:

1. _____

2. _____

Helpful Hints

✓ First, what would be a way to keep yourself calm and in control? (chapter 2)

✓ When he comes home, what communication "do's" can you implement so that you are able to be clear, nonconfrontational, and brief? (chapter 6)

✓ Describe a reward system that you and your son can create together about coming home on time. (chapter 7)

Challenge 6

When you ask your daughter to join a family outing, she says "No way!" and storms up to her bedroom. How could you handle this skillfully?

Your response:

1. _____

2. _____

Helpful Hints

✓ What would be an appropriate "reframe" about growing up and being independent? (chapter 2)

✓ How could you and your spouse/partner support each other in staying calm and using effective parenting skills? (chapter 3)

✓ How can you tell her what you want, instead of asking questions or making accusations? (chapter 6)

✓ Did you remember to impose a consequence for her yelling? (chapter 7)

Challenge 7

You remind your daughter that she has an orthodontist appointment for her braces this afternoon. The appointment conflicts with a play date, and she begins to cry and whine. How could you handle this situation skillfully?

Your response:

1. _____

2. _____

Helpful Hints

✓ First, what would be a humorous exaggeration? For example, "We have to go to the orthodontist so we can get another free toothbrush for our collection!" (chapter 2)

✓ Set a positive tone as an example for your child to model. (chapter 2)

✓ What kind of alternative solution could you and your daughter come up with? For example, maybe she could go to an early orthodontist appointment and then have a play date. (chapter 7)

CONGRATULATIONS ON FINISHING THE SKILLFUL PARENTING CHALLENGE!

For More Help

What should you do if, after all this, you are still feeling stuck parenting your child? How do you know when to seek professional guidance and support? Maybe you feel as though what you are trying isn't working as well as it could. These are some signs that what you're doing isn't working well:

- You're yelling or getting more frustrated than usual.

- Your child continues to misbehave even after you've tried everything.

- There's a change in your child's school performance.

- There's a change in your child's social behavior, like withdrawing from friends or social activities.

- Other people have commented on your child's negative behavior.

If you are concerned, it may be time to seek professional help. The following are the main kinds of professionals in the field.

CLINICAL PSYCHOLOGIST (Ph.D. or Psy.D., doctoral degree)

Child clinical psychologists are experts in children's emotions and behavior. Many years of training prepare them to assess and diagnose psychological problems using specialized testing instruments. Psychologists formulate treatment plans and provide different types of therapy (for example, individual or family therapy).

PSYCHIATRIST (M.D., medical degree)

Child psychiatrists are medical doctors with postgraduate training in abnormal behavior. Training prepares them to assess and diagnose psychiatric problems and to prescribe medication as part of a child's treatment.

CLINICAL SOCIAL WORKER (M.S.W. or C.S.W., master's degree)

Clinical social workers have specialized training in providing case management in home and community settings. They may have additional training in therapy with children, families, and adults.

PSYCHOTHERAPIST (M.S. or M.F.A., master's degree)
A psychotherapist generally has a master's degree in counseling psychology, school psychology, art therapy, or another specific area of psychiatric treatment.

COUNSELOR (bachelor's degree)
A counselor may have a college degree with an additional certificate of training in a specific area, such as substance abuse counseling or domestic violence counseling.

Parenting Posttest

The following parenting quiz will give you a sense of how far you've come. Be honest with yourself—and see how much you have learned! You and your spouse/partner should each complete the quiz separately. When you finish, add up your score using the Scoring Key. Compare your pretest and posttest scores.

Never	Rarely	Sometimes	Frequently	Always
0	**1**	**2**	**3**	**4**

How often do you feel frustrated when you
discipline your child?   _____

How often do you want more time just
for yourself?   _____

How often do you say things to your child that
you later regret?   _____

How often do you and your spouse/partner
disagree about how to raise the children?   _____

How often do you feel undermined by another
adult when you discipline your child?   _____

How often do you wish you had more time with your
spouse/partner to talk about parenting issues?   _____

How often do you have more than three parenting
dilemmas about your child at the same time?   _____

How often do you wish you could deal with parenting
dilemmas more effectively?   _____

How often do you give advice to your child without
being asked for it?   _____

How often do you "lecture" to your child—that is,
talk for at least one minute without stopping?   _____

How often do you say you're going to punish your
child and then give in?   _____

How often does your child lose his/her temper or
become easily frustrated, while you are trying to
discipline him/her?   _____

How often do you get into power struggles with
your children?   _____

How often do you spend less than one hour a day
in conversation with your child?   _____

How often does your child interrupt you and not
give you a chance to explain yourself?   _____

How often do you consider parent-child
communication to be important in your family?   _____

How often do you speak with your child when he/she
is not quite calm enough to listen to you?   _____

How often do you fail to effectively and completely
solve problems with your child?   _____

How often do you come up with only one or two
solutions to a problem? _____

How often do you forget to focus on your
child's strengths? _____

How often is it difficult to spend special quality
time with your child for 15 minutes a day? _____

Scoring Key:
0 – 30
You are a parenting expert. You did a great job practicing the skills outlined in the book. Congratulations!
31 – 50
Though you know a great deal about effective parenting, there are some areas where you could improve your skills. Go back to chapters where you still feel stuck. Congratulate yourself on the areas in which you have improved.
51 – 70
You may find that you are still getting stuck in your parenting. Go back through several chapters, and be sure to involve your parenting partner, use the practice exercises, and be patient. Change can be slow!
71 – 84
Parenting continues to be a challenge for you. It may be time to talk to a professional about parenting issues and to determine whether your child has a behavior disorder. In the meantime, try to focus on the positive, and don't despair—help is available.

Chapter 10

Interactive Family Activities

Make time for fun family activities to promote positive behavior in your children as often as possible. Plan ahead for a brief but enjoyable activity. Here are some suggestions.

Activity 1. Table Time
Play a board game, complete a challenging puzzle, do arts and crafts, build a model, or share another hobby you both enjoy. These can result in hours of naturally flowing conversation.

Activity 2. Cooking a Delicious Meal or Treat Together
Sometimes important topics come up while you are puttering around in the kitchen.

Activity 3. Indoor Group Time
Gather friends and family together for bowling, shopping at the mall, or story time at the library.

Activity 4. Outdoor Group Time
Go to your local playground, play sports at a nearby park; have a picnic; go on a surprise adventure to the zoo, aquarium, or amusement park; or go on a family hike.

Activity 5. Talking Time

Help children identify feelings by using games or books, sing favorite songs together, read books before bed, discuss interesting topics with a teenager, or read the same novel as your teenager and discuss it. Remember, you're not trying to teach your child how to be a better English student. You're just trying to talk.

Activity 6. Memory Lane

Look at baby pictures or childhood videos together as a way to remind children of earlier stages of development.

Activity 7. Getting Involved

Get involved with your child's school. Volunteer to help with extracurricular programs, such as theater or sports. This may help you discover new and exciting characteristics of your child that you would otherwise have missed.

Activity 8. A Family Vacation

This provides a change of scenery and quality bonding time in a fun and relaxing atmosphere.

Conclusion

You've reached the end of the book—HOORAY! Now don't put it away. You never know when you'll need a refresher or booster review. You probably will continue to practice these skills and see successful changes in your children and your family. As one parent recently told us, "Just when I think I have it all figured out, a new challenge presents itself. Luckily, there are other parents who have managed similar challenges and become resources and vehicles for success."

Biographical Information on the Authors

Dr. Lyn Vinnick Kaller is a licensed psychologist who received her Ph.D. in clinical psychology from Virginia Commonwealth University/Medical College of Virginia, with specialized training in child and family therapy. Dr. Kaller has a private practice in Scarsdale, New York, specializing in the treatment of children, teenagers, parents, and families. She was most recently a supervising psychologist in the Outpatient Child and Family Psychiatry Division of St. Luke's-Roosevelt Hospital Center, where she held an appointment as assistant professor of clinical psychology in psychiatry at Columbia University College of Physicians and Surgeons.

Before her work at St. Luke's-Roosevelt Hospital Center, Dr. Kaller was the project director and senior psychologist for a federally funded research treatment program at the Child and Adolescent Behavior Center of Long Island Jewish Medical Center in New York. This included working with children with severe disruptive behavior disorders and their parents, as well as developing parent skills training groups and workshops.

Dr. Kaller is senior author of several psychotherapy treatment manuals, has co-authored book chapters on adolescent suicide and on various therapeutic interventions with children, and has published numerous articles pertaining to children's social skills and childhood disruptive behavior disorders. Dr. Kaller lectures extensively at local schools and community centers and also does television guest appearances. She lives with her husband and daughter in Scarsdale, New York.

Dr. Maria LaPadula Perez is a licensed psychologist who received her Ph.D. in clinical psychology from St. John's University in New York. Currently, she is the coordinator of the Behavioral Sciences Department and assistant professor at the New York Institute of Technology in Old Westbury, New York. Previously, Dr. LaPadula Perez was a senior staff psychologist at the Child and Adolescent Behavior Center of Long Island Jewish Medical Center, treating children and teenagers who had a variety of behavior disorders and assisting with clinical research programs. She has co-authored several psychotherapy treatment manuals and has lectured at local community centers and schools. She lives with her husband and daughter in Glen Head, New York.

Index